FOOD JOURNAL

Breakfast   Servings   Calories

		Subtotal

Snack

		Subtotal

Lunch

		Subtotal

Snack

		Subtotal

Dinner

		Subtotal

Snack

		Subtotal

Total Calories From Food

FITNESS ACTIVITY JOURNAL

     Duration   Calories

Total Calories From Fitness

NOTES

FOOD JOURNAL

Breakfast   Servings   Calories

	Servings	Calories
	Subtotal	

Snack

	Servings	Calories
	Subtotal	

Lunch

	Servings	Calories
	Subtotal	

Snack

	Servings	Calories
	Subtotal	

Dinner

	Servings	Calories
	Subtotal	

Snack

	Servings	Calories
	Subtotal	

Total Calories From Food ____

FITNESS ACTIVITY JOURNAL

	Duration	Calories

Total Calories From Fitness ____

NOTES

_____
_____
_____
_____
_____
_____
_____

FOOD JOURNAL

Breakfast — Servings — Calories

	Servings	Calories
		Subtotal

Snack

	Servings	Calories
		Subtotal

Lunch

	Servings	Calories
		Subtotal

Snack

	Servings	Calories
		Subtotal

Dinner

	Servings	Calories
		Subtotal

Snack

	Servings	Calories
		Subtotal

Total Calories From Food ☐

FITNESS ACTIVITY JOURNAL

	Duration	Calories

Total Calories From Fitness ☐

NOTES

FOOD JOURNAL

Breakfast   **Servings**   **Calories**

	Servings	Calories
	Subtotal	

Snack

	Servings	Calories
	Subtotal	

Lunch

	Servings	Calories
	Subtotal	

Snack

	Servings	Calories
	Subtotal	

Dinner

	Servings	Calories
	Subtotal	

Snack

	Servings	Calories
	Subtotal	

Total Calories From Food [ ]

FITNESS ACTIVITY JOURNAL

	Duration	Calories

Total Calories From Fitness [ ]

NOTES

_____
_____
_____
_____
_____
_____
_____

FOOD JOURNAL

Breakfast — Servings Calories

	Subtotal	

Snack

	Subtotal	

Lunch

	Subtotal	

Snack

	Subtotal	

Dinner

	Subtotal	

Snack

	Subtotal	

Total Calories From Food

FITNESS ACTIVITY JOURNAL

Duration Calories

Total Calories From Fitness

NOTES

FOOD JOURNAL

Breakfast   Servings   Calories

	Servings	Calories
	Subtotal	

Snack

	Servings	Calories
	Subtotal	

Lunch

	Servings	Calories
	Subtotal	

Snack

	Servings	Calories
	Subtotal	

Dinner

	Servings	Calories
	Subtotal	

Snack

	Servings	Calories
	Subtotal	

Total Calories From Food

FITNESS ACTIVITY JOURNAL

	Duration	Calories

Total Calories From Fitness

NOTES

FOOD JOURNAL

Breakfast   Servings   Calories

	Servings	Calories
		Subtotal

Snack

	Servings	Calories
		Subtotal

Lunch

	Servings	Calories
		Subtotal

Snack

	Servings	Calories
		Subtotal

Dinner

	Servings	Calories
		Subtotal

Snack

	Servings	Calories
		Subtotal

Total Calories From Food [ ]

FITNESS ACTIVITY JOURNAL

	Duration	Calories

Total Calories From Fitness [ ]

NOTES

FOOD JOURNAL

Breakfast | **Servings** | **Calories**

| | Subtotal |

Snack

| | Subtotal |

Lunch

| | Subtotal |

Snack

| | Subtotal |

Dinner

| | Subtotal |

Snack

| | Subtotal |

Total Calories From Food

FITNESS ACTIVITY JOURNAL

| | **Duration** | **Calories** |

Total Calories From Fitness

NOTES

FOOD JOURNAL

Breakfast   Servings   Calories

	Servings	Calories
	Subtotal	

Snack

	Servings	Calories
	Subtotal	

Lunch

	Servings	Calories
	Subtotal	

Snack

	Servings	Calories
	Subtotal	

Dinner

	Servings	Calories
	Subtotal	

Snack

	Servings	Calories
	Subtotal	

Total Calories From Food _____

FITNESS ACTIVITY JOURNAL

	Duration	Calories

Total Calories From Fitness _____

NOTES

_____
_____
_____
_____
_____
_____
_____

FOOD JOURNAL

Breakfast | **Servings** | **Calories**

| | Subtotal | |

Snack

| | Subtotal | |

Lunch

| | Subtotal | |

Snack

| | Subtotal | |

Dinner

| | Subtotal | |

Snack

| | Subtotal | |

Total Calories From Food

FITNESS ACTIVITY JOURNAL

| | **Duration** | **Calories** |

Total Calories From Fitness

NOTES

FOOD JOURNAL

Breakfast   Servings Calories

| | Subtotal | |

Snack

| | Subtotal | |

Lunch

| | Subtotal | |

Snack

| | Subtotal | |

Dinner

| | Subtotal | |

Snack

| | Subtotal | |

Total Calories From Food

FITNESS ACTIVITY JOURNAL

Duration   Calories

Total Calories From Fitness

NOTES

FOOD JOURNAL

Breakfast	Servings	Calories
		Subtotal

Snack | |
--- | --- | ---
 | | Subtotal

Lunch | |
--- | --- | ---
 | |
 | |
 | |
 | | Subtotal

Snack | |
--- | --- | ---
 | | Subtotal

Dinner | |
--- | --- | ---
 | |
 | |
 | |
 | | Subtotal

Snack | |
--- | --- | ---
 | | Subtotal

Total Calories From Food

FITNESS ACTIVITY JOURNAL

 | Duration | Calories
--- | --- | ---
 | |
 | |
 | |

Total Calories From Fitness

NOTES

FOOD JOURNAL

Breakfast　　　　　　　　　　　　　　　　Servings　Calories

| | Subtotal | |

Snack

| | Subtotal | |

Lunch

| | Subtotal | |

Snack

| | Subtotal | |

Dinner

| | Subtotal | |

Snack

| | Subtotal | |

Total Calories From Food

FITNESS ACTIVITY JOURNAL

　　　　　　　　　　　　　　　　　　　Duration　　Calories

Total Calories From Fitness

NOTES

FOOD JOURNAL

Breakfast   Servings   Calories

	Subtotal	

Snack

	Subtotal	

Lunch

	Subtotal	

Snack

	Subtotal	

Dinner

	Subtotal	

Snack

	Subtotal	

Total Calories From Food _____

FITNESS ACTIVITY JOURNAL

          Duration   Calories

Total Calories From Fitness _____

NOTES

FOOD JOURNAL

Breakfast   Servings   Calories

	Subtotal	

Snack

	Subtotal	

Lunch

	Subtotal	

Snack

	Subtotal	

Dinner

	Subtotal	

Snack

	Subtotal	

Total Calories From Food ☐

FITNESS ACTIVITY JOURNAL

       Duration   Calories

Total Calories From Fitness ☐

NOTES

FOOD JOURNAL

Breakfast	Servings	Calories
		Subtotal

Snack	Servings	Calories
		Subtotal

Lunch	Servings	Calories
		Subtotal

Snack	Servings	Calories
		Subtotal

Dinner	Servings	Calories
		Subtotal

Snack	Servings	Calories
		Subtotal

Total Calories From Food

FITNESS ACTIVITY JOURNAL

	Duration	Calories

Total Calories From Fitness

NOTES

FOOD JOURNAL

Breakfast   Servings   Calories

	Servings	Calories
		Subtotal

Snack

	Servings	Calories
		Subtotal

Lunch

	Servings	Calories
		Subtotal

Snack

	Servings	Calories
		Subtotal

Dinner

	Servings	Calories
		Subtotal

Snack

	Servings	Calories
		Subtotal

Total Calories From Food [ ]

FITNESS ACTIVITY JOURNAL

	Duration	Calories

Total Calories From Fitness [ ]

NOTES

FOOD JOURNAL

Breakfast   Servings   Calories

	Servings	Calories
	Subtotal	

Snack

	Servings	Calories
	Subtotal	

Lunch

	Servings	Calories
	Subtotal	

Snack

	Servings	Calories
	Subtotal	

Dinner

	Servings	Calories
	Subtotal	

Snack

	Servings	Calories
	Subtotal	

Total Calories From Food [ ]

FITNESS ACTIVITY JOURNAL

	Duration	Calories

Total Calories From Fitness [ ]

NOTES

FOOD JOURNAL

Breakfast   Servings   Calories

	Servings	Calories
		Subtotal

Snack

	Servings	Calories
		Subtotal

Lunch

	Servings	Calories
		Subtotal

Snack

	Servings	Calories
		Subtotal

Dinner

	Servings	Calories
		Subtotal

Snack

	Servings	Calories
		Subtotal

Total Calories From Food [ ]

FITNESS ACTIVITY JOURNAL

	Duration	Calories

Total Calories From Fitness [ ]

NOTES

FOOD JOURNAL

Breakfast	Servings	Calories
		Subtotal

Snack		
		Subtotal

Lunch		
		Subtotal

Snack		
		Subtotal

Dinner		
		Subtotal

Snack		
		Subtotal

Total Calories From Food

FITNESS ACTIVITY JOURNAL

	Duration	Calories

Total Calories From Fitness

NOTES

FOOD JOURNAL

Breakfast   Servings   Calories

	Subtotal	

Snack

	Subtotal	

Lunch

	Subtotal	

Snack

	Subtotal	

Dinner

	Subtotal	

Snack

	Subtotal	

Total Calories From Food

FITNESS ACTIVITY JOURNAL

     Duration   Calories

Total Calories From Fitness

NOTES

FOOD JOURNAL

Breakfast   Servings   Calories

	Servings	Calories
		Subtotal

Snack

	Servings	Calories
		Subtotal

Lunch

	Servings	Calories
		Subtotal

Snack

	Servings	Calories
		Subtotal

Dinner

	Servings	Calories
		Subtotal

Snack

	Servings	Calories
		Subtotal

Total Calories From Food

FITNESS ACTIVITY JOURNAL

	Duration	Calories

Total Calories From Fitness

NOTES

FOOD JOURNAL

Breakfast   Servings   Calories

	Servings	Calories
	Subtotal	

Snack

	Servings	Calories
	Subtotal	

Lunch

	Servings	Calories
	Subtotal	

Snack

	Servings	Calories
	Subtotal	

Dinner

	Servings	Calories
	Subtotal	

Snack

	Servings	Calories
	Subtotal	

Total Calories From Food

FITNESS ACTIVITY JOURNAL

	Duration	Calories

Total Calories From Fitness

NOTES

FOOD JOURNAL

Breakfast | Servings | Calories

		Subtotal

Snack

		Subtotal

Lunch

		Subtotal

Snack

		Subtotal

Dinner

		Subtotal

Snack

		Subtotal

Total Calories From Food

FITNESS ACTIVITY JOURNAL

	Duration	Calories

Total Calories From Fitness

NOTES

FOOD JOURNAL

Breakfast — Servings | Calories

	Servings	Calories
	Subtotal	

Snack

	Servings	Calories
	Subtotal	

Lunch

	Servings	Calories
	Subtotal	

Snack

	Servings	Calories
	Subtotal	

Dinner

	Servings	Calories
	Subtotal	

Snack

	Servings	Calories
	Subtotal	

Total Calories From Food [ ]

FITNESS ACTIVITY JOURNAL

	Duration	Calories

Total Calories From Fitness [ ]

NOTES

FOOD JOURNAL

Breakfast   Servings   Calories

	Servings	Calories
	Subtotal	

Snack

	Servings	Calories
	Subtotal	

Lunch

	Servings	Calories
	Subtotal	

Snack

	Servings	Calories
	Subtotal	

Dinner

	Servings	Calories
	Subtotal	

Snack

	Servings	Calories
	Subtotal	

Total Calories From Food ____

FITNESS ACTIVITY JOURNAL

	Duration	Calories

Total Calories From Fitness ____

NOTES

_____
_____
_____
_____
_____
_____

FOOD JOURNAL

Breakfast   Servings   Calories

	Servings	Calories
		Subtotal

Snack

	Servings	Calories
		Subtotal

Lunch

	Servings	Calories
		Subtotal

Snack

	Servings	Calories
		Subtotal

Dinner

	Servings	Calories
		Subtotal

Snack

	Servings	Calories
		Subtotal

Total Calories From Food ☐

FITNESS ACTIVITY JOURNAL

	Duration	Calories

Total Calories From Fitness ☐

NOTES

_____
_____
_____
_____
_____
_____
_____

FOOD JOURNAL

Breakfast — Servings — Calories

	Servings	Calories
		Subtotal

Snack

	Servings	Calories
		Subtotal

Lunch

	Servings	Calories
		Subtotal

Snack

	Servings	Calories
		Subtotal

Dinner

	Servings	Calories
		Subtotal

Snack

	Servings	Calories
		Subtotal

Total Calories From Food

FITNESS ACTIVITY JOURNAL

	Duration	Calories

Total Calories From Fitness

NOTES

FOOD JOURNAL

Breakfast   Servings   Calories

	Subtotal	

Snack

	Subtotal	

Lunch

	Subtotal	

Snack

	Subtotal	

Dinner

	Subtotal	

Snack

	Subtotal	

Total Calories From Food

FITNESS ACTIVITY JOURNAL

Duration   Calories

Total Calories From Fitness

NOTES

FOOD JOURNAL

Breakfast | **Servings** | **Calories**

		Subtotal

Snack

| | | |
| | | Subtotal |

Lunch

		Subtotal

Snack

| | | |
| | | Subtotal |

Dinner

		Subtotal

Snack

| | | |
| | | Subtotal |

Total Calories From Food

FITNESS ACTIVITY JOURNAL

	Duration	**Calories**

Total Calories From Fitness

NOTES

FOOD JOURNAL

Breakfast   Servings   Calories

	Servings	Calories
		Subtotal

Snack

	Servings	Calories
		Subtotal

Lunch

	Servings	Calories
		Subtotal

Snack

	Servings	Calories
		Subtotal

Dinner

	Servings	Calories
		Subtotal

Snack

	Servings	Calories
		Subtotal

Total Calories From Food [ ]

FITNESS ACTIVITY JOURNAL

	Duration	Calories

Total Calories From Fitness [ ]

NOTES

FOOD JOURNAL

Breakfast   Servings   Calories

	Servings	Calories
	Subtotal	

Snack

	Servings	Calories
	Subtotal	

Lunch

	Servings	Calories
	Subtotal	

Snack

	Servings	Calories
	Subtotal	

Dinner

	Servings	Calories
	Subtotal	

Snack

	Servings	Calories
	Subtotal	

Total Calories From Food _____

FITNESS ACTIVITY JOURNAL

	Duration	Calories

Total Calories From Fitness _____

NOTES

_____
_____
_____
_____
_____
_____

FOOD JOURNAL

Breakfast   Servings   Calories

	Servings	Calories
		Subtotal

Snack

	Servings	Calories
		Subtotal

Lunch

	Servings	Calories
		Subtotal

Snack

	Servings	Calories
		Subtotal

Dinner

	Servings	Calories
		Subtotal

Snack

	Servings	Calories
		Subtotal

Total Calories From Food [ ]

FITNESS ACTIVITY JOURNAL

	Duration	Calories

Total Calories From Fitness [ ]

NOTES

FOOD JOURNAL

Breakfast   Servings   Calories

	Subtotal	

Snack

	Subtotal	

Lunch

	Subtotal	

Snack

	Subtotal	

Dinner

	Subtotal	

Snack

	Subtotal	

Total Calories From Food

FITNESS ACTIVITY JOURNAL

Duration   Calories

Total Calories From Fitness

NOTES

FOOD JOURNAL

Breakfast   Servings   Calories

	Subtotal	

Snack

	Subtotal	

Lunch

	Subtotal	

Snack

	Subtotal	

Dinner

	Subtotal	

Snack

	Subtotal	

Total Calories From Food

FITNESS ACTIVITY JOURNAL

Duration   Calories

Total Calories From Fitness

NOTES

FOOD JOURNAL

Breakfast   Servings   Calories

	Servings	Calories
		Subtotal

Snack

	Servings	Calories
		Subtotal

Lunch

	Servings	Calories
		Subtotal

Snack

	Servings	Calories
		Subtotal

Dinner

	Servings	Calories
		Subtotal

Snack

	Servings	Calories
		Subtotal

Total Calories From Food

FITNESS ACTIVITY JOURNAL

	Duration	Calories

Total Calories From Fitness

NOTES

_____
_____
_____
_____
_____
_____
_____

FOOD JOURNAL

Breakfast   Servings   Calories

	Subtotal	

Snack

	Subtotal	

Lunch

	Subtotal	

Snack

	Subtotal	

Dinner

	Subtotal	

Snack

	Subtotal	

Total Calories From Food

FITNESS ACTIVITY JOURNAL

Duration   Calories

Total Calories From Fitness

NOTES

FOOD JOURNAL

Breakfast | Servings | Calories
	Subtotal

Snack
| | |
| | Subtotal |

Lunch
	Subtotal

Snack
| | |
| | Subtotal |

Dinner
	Subtotal

Snack
| | |
| | Subtotal |

Total Calories From Food

FITNESS ACTIVITY JOURNAL

	Duration	Calories

Total Calories From Fitness

NOTES

FOOD JOURNAL

Breakfast	Servings	Calories
	Subtotal	

Snack		
	Subtotal	

Lunch		
	Subtotal	

Snack		
	Subtotal	

Dinner		
	Subtotal	

Snack		
	Subtotal	

Total Calories From Food

FITNESS ACTIVITY JOURNAL

	Duration	Calories

Total Calories From Fitness

NOTES

FOOD JOURNAL

Breakfast   Servings   Calories

	Servings	Calories
		Subtotal

Snack

	Servings	Calories
		Subtotal

Lunch

	Servings	Calories
		Subtotal

Snack

	Servings	Calories
		Subtotal

Dinner

	Servings	Calories
		Subtotal

Snack

	Servings	Calories
		Subtotal

Total Calories From Food

FITNESS ACTIVITY JOURNAL

	Duration	Calories

Total Calories From Fitness

NOTES

FOOD JOURNAL

Breakfast — Servings — Calories

	Servings	Calories
	Subtotal	

Snack

	Servings	Calories
	Subtotal	

Lunch

	Servings	Calories
	Subtotal	

Snack

	Servings	Calories
	Subtotal	

Dinner

	Servings	Calories
	Subtotal	

Snack

	Servings	Calories
	Subtotal	

Total Calories From Food

FITNESS ACTIVITY JOURNAL

	Duration	Calories

Total Calories From Fitness

NOTES

FOOD JOURNAL

Breakfast | Servings | Calories
	Subtotal

Snack
| | |
| | Subtotal |

Lunch
	Subtotal

Snack
| | |
| | Subtotal |

Dinner
	Subtotal

Snack
| | |
| | Subtotal |

Total Calories From Food

FITNESS ACTIVITY JOURNAL

	Duration	Calories

Total Calories From Fitness

NOTES

FOOD JOURNAL

Breakfast | Servings | Calories
	Subtotal

Snack
| | |
| | Subtotal |

Lunch
	Subtotal

Snack
| | |
| | Subtotal |

Dinner
	Subtotal

Snack
| | |
| | Subtotal |

Total Calories From Food

FITNESS ACTIVITY JOURNAL

	Duration	Calories

Total Calories From Fitness

NOTES

FOOD JOURNAL

Breakfast   Servings   Calories

	Servings	Calories
	Subtotal	

Snack

	Servings	Calories
	Subtotal	

Lunch

	Servings	Calories
	Subtotal	

Snack

	Servings	Calories
	Subtotal	

Dinner

	Servings	Calories
	Subtotal	

Snack

	Servings	Calories
	Subtotal	

Total Calories From Food

FITNESS ACTIVITY JOURNAL

	Duration	Calories

Total Calories From Fitness

NOTES

FOOD JOURNAL

Breakfast　　　　　　　　　　　　　　　　Servings　Calories

| | Subtotal | |

Snack

| | Subtotal | |

Lunch

| | Subtotal | |

Snack

| | Subtotal | |

Dinner

| | Subtotal | |

Snack

| | Subtotal | |

Total Calories From Food

FITNESS ACTIVITY JOURNAL

　　　　　　　　　　　　　　　　　　　　　　Duration　Calories

Total Calories From Fitness

NOTES

FOOD JOURNAL

Breakfast   **Servings**   **Calories**

	Servings	Calories
		Subtotal

Snack

	Servings	Calories
		Subtotal

Lunch

	Servings	Calories
		Subtotal

Snack

	Servings	Calories
		Subtotal

Dinner

	Servings	Calories
		Subtotal

Snack

	Servings	Calories
		Subtotal

Total Calories From Food [ ]

FITNESS ACTIVITY JOURNAL

	Duration	Calories

Total Calories From Fitness [ ]

NOTES

_____
_____
_____
_____
_____
_____

FOOD JOURNAL

Breakfast   Servings   Calories

	Servings	Calories
	Subtotal	

Snack

	Servings	Calories
	Subtotal	

Lunch

	Servings	Calories
	Subtotal	

Snack

	Servings	Calories
	Subtotal	

Dinner

	Servings	Calories
	Subtotal	

Snack

	Servings	Calories
	Subtotal	

Total Calories From Food

FITNESS ACTIVITY JOURNAL

	Duration	Calories

Total Calories From Fitness

NOTES

FOOD JOURNAL

Breakfast | Servings | Calories
	Subtotal

Snack
| | |
| | Subtotal |

Lunch
	Subtotal

Snack
| | |
| | Subtotal |

Dinner
	Subtotal

Snack
| | |
| | Subtotal |

Total Calories From Food

FITNESS ACTIVITY JOURNAL

	Duration	Calories

Total Calories From Fitness

NOTES

FOOD JOURNAL

Breakfast   Servings   Calories

	Subtotal	

Snack

	Subtotal	

Lunch

	Subtotal	

Snack

	Subtotal	

Dinner

	Subtotal	

Snack

	Subtotal	

Total Calories From Food

FITNESS ACTIVITY JOURNAL

Duration   Calories

Total Calories From Fitness

NOTES

FOOD JOURNAL

Breakfast   Servings   Calories

| | Subtotal | |

Snack

| | Subtotal | |

Lunch

| | Subtotal | |

Snack

| | Subtotal | |

Dinner

| | Subtotal | |

Snack

| | Subtotal | |

Total Calories From Food

FITNESS ACTIVITY JOURNAL

     Duration   Calories

Total Calories From Fitness

NOTES

FOOD JOURNAL

Breakfast   Servings   Calories

	Subtotal	

Snack

	Subtotal	

Lunch

	Subtotal	

Snack

	Subtotal	

Dinner

	Subtotal	

Snack

	Subtotal	

Total Calories From Food

FITNESS ACTIVITY JOURNAL

     Duration   Calories

Total Calories From Fitness

NOTES

FOOD JOURNAL

Breakfast | **Servings** | **Calories**

| | Subtotal | |

Snack

| | Subtotal | |

Lunch

| | Subtotal | |

Snack

| | Subtotal | |

Dinner

| | Subtotal | |

Snack

| | Subtotal | |

Total Calories From Food

FITNESS ACTIVITY JOURNAL

| | **Duration** | **Calories** |

Total Calories From Fitness

NOTES

FOOD JOURNAL

Breakfast	Servings	Calories
	Subtotal	

Snack		
	Subtotal	

Lunch		
	Subtotal	

Snack		
	Subtotal	

Dinner		
	Subtotal	

Snack		
	Subtotal	

Total Calories From Food ☐

FITNESS ACTIVITY JOURNAL

	Duration	Calories

Total Calories From Fitness ☐

NOTES

FOOD JOURNAL

Breakfast | **Servings** | **Calories**
		Subtotal

Snack
| | | |
| | | Subtotal |

Lunch
		Subtotal

Snack
| | | |
| | | Subtotal |

Dinner
		Subtotal

Snack
| | | |
| | | Subtotal |

Total Calories From Food

FITNESS ACTIVITY JOURNAL

	Duration	Calories

Total Calories From Fitness

NOTES

FOOD JOURNAL

Breakfast | Servings | Calories
	Subtotal

Snack
| | |
| | Subtotal |

Lunch
	Subtotal

Snack
| | |
| | Subtotal |

Dinner
	Subtotal

Snack
| | |
| | Subtotal |

Total Calories From Food

FITNESS ACTIVITY JOURNAL

	Duration	Calories

Total Calories From Fitness

NOTES

FOOD JOURNAL

Breakfast   Servings   Calories

	Servings	Calories
	Subtotal	

Snack

	Servings	Calories
	Subtotal	

Lunch

	Servings	Calories
	Subtotal	

Snack

	Servings	Calories
	Subtotal	

Dinner

	Servings	Calories
	Subtotal	

Snack

	Servings	Calories
	Subtotal	

Total Calories From Food [ ]

FITNESS ACTIVITY JOURNAL

	Duration	Calories

Total Calories From Fitness [ ]

NOTES

_____
_____
_____
_____
_____
_____
_____

FOOD JOURNAL

Breakfast — Servings — Calories

	Servings	Calories
	Subtotal	

Snack

	Servings	Calories
	Subtotal	

Lunch

	Servings	Calories
	Subtotal	

Snack

	Servings	Calories
	Subtotal	

Dinner

	Servings	Calories
	Subtotal	

Snack

	Servings	Calories
	Subtotal	

Total Calories From Food

FITNESS ACTIVITY JOURNAL

	Duration	Calories

Total Calories From Fitness

NOTES

FOOD JOURNAL

Breakfast	Servings	Calories
		Subtotal

Snack		
		Subtotal

Lunch		
		Subtotal

Snack		
		Subtotal

Dinner		
		Subtotal

Snack		
		Subtotal

Total Calories From Food

FITNESS ACTIVITY JOURNAL

	Duration	Calories

Total Calories From Fitness

NOTES

FOOD JOURNAL

Breakfast   Servings   Calories

	Subtotal	

Snack

	Subtotal	

Lunch

	Subtotal	

Snack

	Subtotal	

Dinner

	Subtotal	

Snack

	Subtotal	

Total Calories From Food

FITNESS ACTIVITY JOURNAL

     Duration   Calories

Total Calories From Fitness

NOTES

FOOD JOURNAL

Breakfast | **Servings** | **Calories**
	Subtotal

Snack
| | |
| | **Subtotal** |

Lunch
	Subtotal

Snack
| | |
| | **Subtotal** |

Dinner
	Subtotal

Snack
| | |
| | **Subtotal** |

Total Calories From Food

FITNESS ACTIVITY JOURNAL

	Duration	**Calories**

Total Calories From Fitness

NOTES

Habit Tracker

Month _____

Year _____

Day													
1													
2													
3													
4													
5													
6													
7													
8													
9													
10													
11													
12													
13													
14													
15													
16													
17													
18													
19													
20													
21													
22													
23													
24													
25													
26													
27													
28													
29													
30													
31													

Habit Tracker

Month _____

Year _____

Day												
1												
2												
3												
4												
5												
6												
7												
8												
9												
10												
11												
12												
13												
14												
15												
16												
17												
18												
19												
20												
21												
22												
23												
24												
25												
26												
27												
28												
29												
30												
31												

Habit Tracker

Month _____

Year _____

Day													
1													
2													
3													
4													
5													
6													
7													
8													
9													
10													
11													
12													
13													
14													
15													
16													
17													
18													
19													
20													
21													
22													
23													
24													
25													
26													
27													
28													
29													
30													
31													

Habit Tracker

Month _____
Year _____

Day											
1											
2											
3											
4											
5											
6											
7											
8											
9											
10											
11											
12											
13											
14											
15											
16											
17											
18											
19											
20											
21											
22											
23											
24											
25											
26											
27											
28											
29											
30											
31											

Habit Tracker

Month _____

Year _____

Day														
1														
2														
3														
4														
5														
6														
7														
8														
9														
10														
11														
12														
13														
14														
15														
16														
17														
18														
19														
20														
21														
22														
23														
24														
25														
26														
27														
28														
29														
30														
31														

Habit Tracker Month _____

Year _____

Day

1
2
3
4
5
6
7
8
9
10
11
12
13
14
15
16
17
18
19
20
21
22
23
24
25
26
27
28
29
30
31

Habit Tracker

Month _____

Year _____

Day

1														
2														
3														
4														
5														
6														
7														
8														
9														
10														
11														
12														
13														
14														
15														
16														
17														
18														
19														
20														
21														
22														
23														
24														
25														
26														
27														
28														
29														
30														
31														

Habit Tracker

Month _____

Year _____

Day											
1											
2											
3											
4											
5											
6											
7											
8											
9											
10											
11											
12											
13											
14											
15											
16											
17											
18											
19											
20											
21											
22											
23											
24											
25											
26											
27											
28											
29											
30											
31											

Habit Tracker

Month _____

Year _____

Day													
1													
2													
3													
4													
5													
6													
7													
8													
9													
10													
11													
12													
13													
14													
15													
16													
17													
18													
19													
20													
21													
22													
23													
24													
25													
26													
27													
28													
29													
30													
31													

Habit Tracker

Month _____

Year _____

Day													
1													
2													
3													
4													
5													
6													
7													
8													
9													
10													
11													
12													
13													
14													
15													
16													
17													
18													
19													
20													
21													
22													
23													
24													
25													
26													
27													
28													
29													
30													
31													

Habit Tracker

Month _____

Year _____

Day											
1											
2											
3											
4											
5											
6											
7											
8											
9											
10											
11											
12											
13											
14											
15											
16											
17											
18											
19											
20											
21											
22											
23											
24											
25											
26											
27											
28											
29											
30											
31											

Habit Tracker

Month _____

Year _____

Day													
1													
2													
3													
4													
5													
6													
7													
8													
9													
10													
11													
12													
13													
14													
15													
16													
17													
18													
19													
20													
21													
22													
23													
24													
25													
26													
27													
28													
29													
30													
31													

Habit Tracker

Month _____

Year _____

Day													
1													
2													
3													
4													
5													
6													
7													
8													
9													
10													
11													
12													
13													
14													
15													
16													
17													
18													
19													
20													
21													
22													
23													
24													
25													
26													
27													
28													
29													
30													
31													

Habit Tracker

Month _____

Year _____

Day												
1												
2												
3												
4												
5												
6												
7												
8												
9												
10												
11												
12												
13												
14												
15												
16												
17												
18												
19												
20												
21												
22												
23												
24												
25												
26												
27												
28												
29												
30												
31												

Habit Tracker

Month _____

Year _____

Day														
1														
2														
3														
4														
5														
6														
7														
8														
9														
10														
11														
12														
13														
14														
15														
16														
17														
18														
19														
20														
21														
22														
23														
24														
25														
26														
27														
28														
29														
30														
31														

Habit Tracker

Month _____

Year _____

Day													
1													
2													
3													
4													
5													
6													
7													
8													
9													
10													
11													
12													
13													
14													
15													
16													
17													
18													
19													
20													
21													
22													
23													
24													
25													
26													
27													
28													
29													
30													
31													

Habit Tracker Month _____

Year _____

Day											
1											
2											
3											
4											
5											
6											
7											
8											
9											
10											
11											
12											
13											
14											
15											
16											
17											
18											
19											
20											
21											
22											
23											
24											
25											
26											
27											
28											
29											
30											
31											

Habit Tracker Month _____
 Year _____

Day												
1												
2												
3												
4												
5												
6												
7												
8												
9												
10												
11												
12												
13												
14												
15												
16												
17												
18												
19												
20												
21												
22												
23												
24												
25												
26												
27												
28												
29												
30												
31												

Habit Tracker

Month _____

Year _____

Day												
1												
2												
3												
4												
5												
6												
7												
8												
9												
10												
11												
12												
13												
14												
15												
16												
17												
18												
19												
20												
21												
22												
23												
24												
25												
26												
27												
28												
29												
30												
31												

Habit Tracker   Month _____

                          Year _____

Day													
1													
2													
3													
4													
5													
6													
7													
8													
9													
10													
11													
12													
13													
14													
15													
16													
17													
18													
19													
20													
21													
22													
23													
24													
25													
26													
27													
28													
29													
30													
31													

Habit Tracker

Month _____

Year _____

Day											
1											
2											
3											
4											
5											
6											
7											
8											
9											
10											
11											
12											
13											
14											
15											
16											
17											
18											
19											
20											
21											
22											
23											
24											
25											
26											
27											
28											
29											
30											
31											

Habit Tracker

Month _____

Year _____

Day												
1												
2												
3												
4												
5												
6												
7												
8												
9												
10												
11												
12												
13												
14												
15												
16												
17												
18												
19												
20												
21												
22												
23												
24												
25												
26												
27												
28												
29												
30												
31												

Habit Tracker

Month _____

Year _____

Day													
1													
2													
3													
4													
5													
6													
7													
8													
9													
10													
11													
12													
13													
14													
15													
16													
17													
18													
19													
20													
21													
22													
23													
24													
25													
26													
27													
28													
29													
30													
31													

Habit Tracker

Month _____

Year _____

Day

1											
2											
3											
4											
5											
6											
7											
8											
9											
10											
11											
12											
13											
14											
15											
16											
17											
18											
19											
20											
21											
22											
23											
24											
25											
26											
27											
28											
29											
30											
31											

Habit Tracker   Month _____

                           Year _____

Day

1												
2												
3												
4												
5												
6												
7												
8												
9												
10												
11												
12												
13												
14												
15												
16												
17												
18												
19												
20												
21												
22												
23												
24												
25												
26												
27												
28												
29												
30												
31												

Habit Tracker

Month _____

Year _____

Day

Habit Tracker

Month _____

Year _____

Day												
1												
2												
3												
4												
5												
6												
7												
8												
9												
10												
11												
12												
13												
14												
15												
16												
17												
18												
19												
20												
21												
22												
23												
24												
25												
26												
27												
28												
29												
30												
31												

Habit Tracker

Month _____

Year _____

Day

1													
2													
3													
4													
5													
6													
7													
8													
9													
10													
11													
12													
13													
14													
15													
16													
17													
18													
19													
20													
21													
22													
23													
24													
25													
26													
27													
28													
29													
30													
31													

Habit Tracker

Month _____

Year _____

Day													
1													
2													
3													
4													
5													
6													
7													
8													
9													
10													
11													
12													
13													
14													
15													
16													
17													
18													
19													
20													
21													
22													
23													
24													
25													
26													
27													
28													
29													
30													
31													

Habit Tracker

Month _____

Year _____

Day

1													
2													
3													
4													
5													
6													
7													
8													
9													
10													
11													
12													
13													
14													
15													
16													
17													
18													
19													
20													
21													
22													
23													
24													
25													
26													
27													
28													
29													
30													
31													

Habit Tracker

Month _____

Year _____

Day

1												
2												
3												
4												
5												
6												
7												
8												
9												
10												
11												
12												
13												
14												
15												
16												
17												
18												
19												
20												
21												
22												
23												
24												
25												
26												
27												
28												
29												
30												
31												

Habit Tracker

Month _____

Year _____

Day														
1														
2														
3														
4														
5														
6														
7														
8														
9														
10														
11														
12														
13														
14														
15														
16														
17														
18														
19														
20														
21														
22														
23														
24														
25														
26														
27														
28														
29														
30														
31														

Habit Tracker

Month _____

Year _____

Day												
1												
2												
3												
4												
5												
6												
7												
8												
9												
10												
11												
12												
13												
14												
15												
16												
17												
18												
19												
20												
21												
22												
23												
24												
25												
26												
27												
28												
29												
30												
31												

Habit Tracker

Month _____

Year _____

Day												
1												
2												
3												
4												
5												
6												
7												
8												
9												
10												
11												
12												
13												
14												
15												
16												
17												
18												
19												
20												
21												
22												
23												
24												
25												
26												
27												
28												
29												
30												
31												

Habit Tracker

Month _____

Year _____

Day

1														
2														
3														
4														
5														
6														
7														
8														
9														
10														
11														
12														
13														
14														
15														
16														
17														
18														
19														
20														
21														
22														
23														
24														
25														
26														
27														
28														
29														
30														
31														

Habit Tracker Month _____

Year _____

Day

1												
2												
3												
4												
5												
6												
7												
8												
9												
10												
11												
12												
13												
14												
15												
16												
17												
18												
19												
20												
21												
22												
23												
24												
25												
26												
27												
28												
29												
30												
31												

Habit Tracker

Month _____

Year _____

Day													
1													
2													
3													
4													
5													
6													
7													
8													
9													
10													
11													
12													
13													
14													
15													
16													
17													
18													
19													
20													
21													
22													
23													
24													
25													
26													
27													
28													
29													
30													
31													

Habit Tracker

Month _____

Year _____

Day

Habit Tracker

Month _____

Year _____

Day												
1												
2												
3												
4												
5												
6												
7												
8												
9												
10												
11												
12												
13												
14												
15												
16												
17												
18												
19												
20												
21												
22												
23												
24												
25												
26												
27												
28												
29												
30												
31												

Habit Tracker

Month _____

Year _____

Day

1											
2											
3											
4											
5											
6											
7											
8											
9											
10											
11											
12											
13											
14											
15											
16											
17											
18											
19											
20											
21											
22											
23											
24											
25											
26											
27											
28											
29											
30											
31											

Habit Tracker

Month _____

Year _____

Day

1											
2											
3											
4											
5											
6											
7											
8											
9											
10											
11											
12											
13											
14											
15											
16											
17											
18											
19											
20											
21											
22											
23											
24											
25											
26											
27											
28											
29											
30											
31											

Habit Tracker

Month _____

Year _____

Day												
1												
2												
3												
4												
5												
6												
7												
8												
9												
10												
11												
12												
13												
14												
15												
16												
17												
18												
19												
20												
21												
22												
23												
24												
25												
26												
27												
28												
29												
30												
31												

Habit Tracker

Month _____
Year _____

Day													
1													
2													
3													
4													
5													
6													
7													
8													
9													
10													
11													
12													
13													
14													
15													
16													
17													
18													
19													
20													
21													
22													
23													
24													
25													
26													
27													
28													
29													
30													
31													

Habit Tracker Month _____

Year _____

Day

1
2
3
4
5
6
7
8
9
10
11
12
13
14
15
16
17
18
19
20
21
22
23
24
25
26
27
28
29
30
31

Habit Tracker

Month _____

Year _____

Day

1											
2											
3											
4											
5											
6											
7											
8											
9											
10											
11											
12											
13											
14											
15											
16											
17											
18											
19											
20											
21											
22											
23											
24											
25											
26											
27											
28											
29											
30											
31											

Habit Tracker

Month _____

Year _____

Day

1													
2													
3													
4													
5													
6													
7													
8													
9													
10													
11													
12													
13													
14													
15													
16													
17													
18													
19													
20													
21													
22													
23													
24													
25													
26													
27													
28													
29													
30													
31													

Habit Tracker

Month _____

Year _____

Day												
1												
2												
3												
4												
5												
6												
7												
8												
9												
10												
11												
12												
13												
14												
15												
16												
17												
18												
19												
20												
21												
22												
23												
24												
25												
26												
27												
28												
29												
30												
31												

Habit Tracker

Month _____

Year _____

Day										
1										
2										
3										
4										
5										
6										
7										
8										
9										
10										
11										
12										
13										
14										
15										
16										
17										
18										
19										
20										
21										
22										
23										
24										
25										
26										
27										
28										
29										
30										
31										

Habit Tracker

Month _____

Year _____

Day													
1													
2													
3													
4													
5													
6													
7													
8													
9													
10													
11													
12													
13													
14													
15													
16													
17													
18													
19													
20													
21													
22													
23													
24													
25													
26													
27													
28													
29													
30													
31													

Habit Tracker

Month _____

Year _____

Day												
1												
2												
3												
4												
5												
6												
7												
8												
9												
10												
11												
12												
13												
14												
15												
16												
17												
18												
19												
20												
21												
22												
23												
24												
25												
26												
27												
28												
29												
30												
31												

Habit Tracker

Month _____

Year _____

Day													
1													
2													
3													
4													
5													
6													
7													
8													
9													
10													
11													
12													
13													
14													
15													
16													
17													
18													
19													
20													
21													
22													
23													
24													
25													
26													
27													
28													
29													
30													
31													

Habit Tracker

Month _____

Year _____

Day

1											
2											
3											
4											
5											
6											
7											
8											
9											
10											
11											
12											
13											
14											
15											
16											
17											
18											
19											
20											
21											
22											
23											
24											
25											
26											
27											
28											
29											
30											
31											

Habit Tracker

Month _____

Year _____

Day														
1														
2														
3														
4														
5														
6														
7														
8														
9														
10														
11														
12														
13														
14														
15														
16														
17														
18														
19														
20														
21														
22														
23														
24														
25														
26														
27														
28														
29														
30														
31														

Habit Tracker

Month _____

Year _____

Day

1												
2												
3												
4												
5												
6												
7												
8												
9												
10												
11												
12												
13												
14												
15												
16												
17												
18												
19												
20												
21												
22												
23												
24												
25												
26												
27												
28												
29												
30												
31												

Habit Tracker

Month _____

Year _____

Day													
1													
2													
3													
4													
5													
6													
7													
8													
9													
10													
11													
12													
13													
14													
15													
16													
17													
18													
19													
20													
21													
22													
23													
24													
25													
26													
27													
28													
29													
30													
31													

Habit Tracker

Month _____

Year _____

Day

1												
2												
3												
4												
5												
6												
7												
8												
9												
10												
11												
12												
13												
14												
15												
16												
17												
18												
19												
20												
21												
22												
23												
24												
25												
26												
27												
28												
29												
30												
31												

Habit Tracker

Month _____

Year _____

Day												
1												
2												
3												
4												
5												
6												
7												
8												
9												
10												
11												
12												
13												
14												
15												
16												
17												
18												
19												
20												
21												
22												
23												
24												
25												
26												
27												
28												
29												
30												
31												

Habit Tracker

Month _____

Year _____

Day

	1
	2
	3
	4
	5
	6
	7
	8
	9
	10
	11
	12
	13
	14
	15
	16
	17
	18
	19
	20
	21
	22
	23
	24
	25
	26
	27
	28
	29
	30
	31

Habit Tracker

Month _____

Year _____

Day												
1												
2												
3												
4												
5												
6												
7												
8												
9												
10												
11												
12												
13												
14												
15												
16												
17												
18												
19												
20												
21												
22												
23												
24												
25												
26												
27												
28												
29												
30												
31												

Habit Tracker

Month _____
Year _____

Day												
1												
2												
3												
4												
5												
6												
7												
8												
9												
10												
11												
12												
13												
14												
15												
16												
17												
18												
19												
20												
21												
22												
23												
24												
25												
26												
27												
28												
29												
30												
31												

www.ingramcontent.com/pod-product-compliance
Lightning Source LLC
LaVergne TN
LVHW012114070526
838202LV00056B/5736